NOW THAT YOU KNOW

Shakendra D. Fullmore

ISBN: 978-0-578-50633-3

Contents

Acknowledgments

I give honor to God for all that he has done and doing in my Life. My marvelous parents Robin Epps-Greene (Melvin), Kenyatt Fullmore (Aundreal), & Carl Kincade. The brilliant siblings- Carlas (Caree) Kincade, Caleb Kincade, Jamarcus Key, and one and only sister Precious Fullmore. I want to thank my grandmothers Catherine Epps & Helen Wright for their great love, listening ears, and encouragement. My precious great-grandmother Elizabeth (Betty) Jones; a jewel of wisdom. All my aunts, uncles, & cousins which are a million in one. A family that prays together stays together, and I love you all more than words could express. The role of Pastorship is not an easy one; I want to thank God for creating you to guide me with his word, Apostle Gossipya Makinwa & girls Chloe and Olive; much love. To my guardian angel, my dearest, & best friend for life Breanna Tippins S.I.P (sleep in peace) I love you and miss you so much. A very humble and sweet vessel Pastor Twila Johnson I honor you for your last night talks, nurturing words, delicious treats, soulful food and loving spirit. Lifetime friends and family Quarry and Bryanna Johnson I thank you all for always hearing me out, being a helping hand, shoulder to lean/cry on, and believing in me. Overall gratitude to family and friends for all the congratulations, thank yous, encouraging words, prayers, and texts/calls.

NOW THAT YOU KNOW

.

Chapter 1
Test

Note: This isn't a standard book. The dialogue is similar to a pep talk/letter/text msgs (you know when you are trying to let your girls, bros, peoples get all the tea). Do NOT read it as a novel.

Life has many knocks and bumps. Right? I know, but it's LIFE, and it doesn't stop. I'll tell you I wanted to throw in the towel so many times, but that's not an option. I must say it get ugly before it gets pretty. Right?? After we get on track and do what is required of us rather that's being a recovering drug addict, a faithful wife/ husband, or even accepting your ministry, there are still trials and tribulations that may come your way. Through the gray areas, there is yet another birth in you. When all hope is gone where do you turn just when you thought it was over what do you do? Huh?? Well, I was once there too. Sometimes you get tired, but everything in you won't let you give in. It's a struggle, but when you know who you are you STILL stand.

After I faced those things back in 2011-2017 discussed in Book 1 "I'm that Girl Only If You Knew" previously, God took complete control. I didn't know a test was approaching in my faith and growth. Returning to Atlanta had me in a new place, although I was there off and on eight years; it was very different. I started working with an excellent job.

However, it was the beginning of my test. How many of you been tested before? One you think you got all under control, too. The new job was everything, money good, hours great, and coworkers as well. Things began to turn immediately advancing me to a different depth in life; I never thought I'd face. I got complacent not following the command God gave me concerning writing my first book "I'm that Girl, Only If You Knew." I was doing what Kendra wanted to — resulting in a resignation soon after getting my feet wet in my career; poppin' and my getting apartment together. I couldn't figure out why? Why me Lord? I had bills and needs; I wanted to shop & travel, have fun; my credit was going to be ruin. I asked all these questions although I knew the answer. I could not see the big picture. I just wanted to do me. How many of you know God moves us in and out of places to learn, advance, and progress? Sometimes he moves us out the way to give us better, then before. And that's exactly what he was doing for me. But we must be meek and prepared if we want to pass the test. Because of the next time around may be a challenge. It seemed like everything in my life was different. Can you trust the shift? As many say "trust the process" that's the hardest part about it all. It's always something great waiting when you least expect it.

Chapter 2
Submission

After resigning from my job, I gave up on every dream I wanted to make a reality. One month of unemployment turn into three-months, I was the process of publishing my first book. And boy was I over it. I was following God's instructions, but my life was in shambles, I thought. Here I was being obedient but low. I was at the most inferior valley life may bring, I thought. I gave in, still in doubt became fearful and lost track. I wanted a job I didn't want to sit at home doing anything. I worried tremendously about my money everything I needed. I knew I had to get back on my feet. I had to push everything in me OUT. Then, I submitted the test. I released my book by hosting a signing I was nervous; I was timid— the book very transparent no secrets and straight forward. I felt so nervous because I was scared to share what I endured. My questions were, "What would others think of me and What will I gain or lose?"

However, it was all in God's plan. My story inspired so many people — that was my strength. After the signing, I was still unemployed sitting in the housing doing absolutely nothing except going to church just the typical traits of a boring life. Two months passed no love life, no job, no social life. But, remember as I stated before God was preparing me for the shift. Five months still on the couch from doing homework— working on my MBA, being around family, to attending church, and trying to wait on good acts. I applied to jobs every day, but nothing happened.

One day I received a call back from 3 jobs I interviewed for all still yet no offer. I started losing hope. I went into a deep depression. I just wanted to sit in the room. I started thinking about all the good and the bad. Nobody or nothing could make me feel happy about my life. Nothing major was happening for me. The book sales were okay, but not enough.

Later, I got an invite on my hometown (Jesup, GA) radio show WIFCO 105.5 Big Dog Country to discuss "I'm that Girl, Only If You Knew." I felt much better weeks passed money was getting tight, and I started losing myself. Then I received good news my book it got approved by the school board members in my hometown for middle and high school. That's when I began to understand everything is on God's timing. I need to realize I need to be patient. The ship was coming for me; it wasn't over.

Furthermore, two weeks later three jobs called for me boy was I happy. I instantly got on the road from my parents' house to return to Atlanta, GA. I interview for the Paralegal position as the Law Firm. The interview went great, and oh man was I waiting on a callback.

Chapter 3
Open Doors

I waited and waited for a response from the firm; I just knew I had the job. Meanwhile, I continued to apply for jobs day after day. The firm never called I started to fret and doubt. I worried myself while pretending to be as happy as I would be. One day on a Monday I received a call for a job (a non-profit co.) The Human Resources manager asked if I would be able to come in for an interview. I assured her I was available immediately. The next morning, I interviewed for the position; this job was nowhere near my undergrad degree. It was related to my MBA; I was in for a new treat. I was nervous but ready to learn something new, anything to get me out of the house. The interview was two hours with many assessment tests; I was beyond ready to leave. Upon completion, the Director informed me there were more candidates to interview.

When I returned home, I began to read my Bible asking God to open doors that no man could shut. In this new experience, God was trying to open my eyes to watch. Later, that day I attended bible study the topic was Trusting God. The word was clear God was speaking to me. It was what I needed to hear direct confirmation.

Bible study ended at about 8 p.m. My phone began to ring; I looked at the number I didn't recognize it. I thought to myself shall I answer or perhaps it's a telemarketer. Then, I heard a still voice (God) telling me to answer the phone. I finally picked up the call. It was the Director of the non-profit. She said may I speak with Ms. Fullmore. I replied This is she. She stated the CFO (Chief Financial Officer), and I have decided to offer you the position, but we changed it to an internship. Are you still interested? I almost busted into tears, lost for word replying yes, I am beyond interested. The entire time I thought it was all over for me. God had a plan for me. He never left "Jesus Christ is the same yesterday and today and forever "Hebrew 13:8 NIV. He came right on time; In life, we must lean on him when think it's bad it may be for good. God wants us to "Trust in the Lord with all thine heart and lean not unto thine own understanding. In all thy ways acknowledge him, and he shall direct thy paths." Proverbs 3:5-6 KIV

I felt a great relieve in my heart, body, and soul. I began to give God thanks for everything. We must crawl before we can walk. The test was over; he was sending me to the organization with a purpose. I was following his lead on this path. Thursday, I attended my first day of work being very observant. I began to reason about me being there. Friday, the company hosted a luncheon for a mentoring program for young girls. The staff invited me. I was intrigued because empowering girls is my passion. The gathering was their first meeting they wanted me to become a mentor and share my story.I didn't want to move. I could hear God say, "Kendra get up!" I was fighting within myself; I stood up my nerves were wrecked and began to speak, tears started falling. I was in the right place at the right time. God wanted me to help the next person.

After, the occasion people wanted advice, my book, and a connection. God lead me there, but the work was over. It was a temporarily just for a season. The weekend was approaching. I rested and slept like a baby. Monday morning, I attended work as usual. Later in the week, a met an older woman in my department. I kept watching her. I was unsure of her spirit; I watched her daily. Soon she began to talk to me; I was impressed. Then the dialogue shift we began to talk about God. Oh boy!! I was listening; she was unfolding everything about ministry. I had all my ears. She soon started on experiences I faced no one knew at this job. This woman didn't know me from Adam's apple. We talked and talked I didn't want to leave work. A week went by every day I was itching to get to work to speak with her just her presence.

I began to ask God, what are you doing? He soon made me realize I sent you to this place at this time for this woman. He said I need you to give her some guidance and the word through me. And she a tool to help you with some things in your career and to stay focused. Every day of work was life my secret place in my prayer closet, hearing what I needed and wanted. I received it all much encouragement in that season for my life.

It amazes me how we meet people who are genuine and pure wholehearted. My spirit grew more and more, but it was a two-fold effect. To prosper always remember to sow into others. I learned we could not receive and not sow back. Meeting this lady, I planted into her and vice versa. When we speak into people lives, there should always be a return because if we empty, we are weak and dry spiritually. In life, we must pour out and fill our spirit back up.

My time was coming to an end at this job. God was getting me ready to move me, I sensed it, but when? I had no idea. I knew I had to apply to a stable job. I began the process again interview after interview. Lastly, I interview for a position at a firm not knowing the position was mines. The meeting wasn't an interview; it was an introduction to the firm. My new journey at the firm was on the 40th floor. When I left, I got in the elevator and started praising on my long way down to the lobby. After eight months of continuously believing in God's word and promises and also in the mist I kept praying. Prayer is the number one key to get us our breakthrough, two fasting and three believing fully trusting God. I finally got my breakthrough.

I needed to surrender all and trust. In many situations, we put our hand in it, but we cannot we got to back up let go and let God do the work. See, it is hard sometimes because we enter a gray area of our lives which is the middle. We cannot see past it. We focused on the past all the good how this happened, how we had this or that, when/what we had, and last how we can get what we need. But in the middle, we got to trust what we're expecting in the end. Speak life, call those things forth as though they are. As it is written: "I have made you a father of many nations." He is our father in the sight of God, in whom he believed—the God who gives life to the dead and calls into being things that were not. Against all hope, Abraham in hope believed and so he became the father of many nations, just as it had been said to him, "So shall your offspring be." Romans 4:17-18 NIV Speak it into existence, meditate on it, and act. Faith without works is dead. "Now faith is the substance of things hoped for, the evidence of things not seen." Hebrews 11:1 KJV

We got to push forward, press, and react! Everything that occurs happens for a reason and a season. We must realize our position in seasons so that we may flourish. Some occurrences aren't for some seasons that may be for another. Our gifts are limited when we aren't equipped in our seasons. We are likely to lose it all because we need spiritual tools. The key is to wait it's a challenge, but we shall to receive the full blessing not half of it, just like ATM (All the Money).

Chapter 4
Winner

As I sit back and reflect on my life the good, bad, pretty and the ugly, the mistakes which were lesson teachers it was motivation for a higher level. I realize I cannot do anything without moving in faith. I said MOVING IN FAITH. React with expectation and progression. Every day we wake up is a test on the job, our spouse, with the kids, family, friends, and even in our faith. In every race there is a finish line; it's not who finishes the fastest. It's about who has the most breath when they finish. Who wants to finish the race dead?? While going through the race we're going to have some setbacks, temptations, and bad days. At the end of it all, we can celebrate not because we finish, but we have the breath of life; we are the WINNER.

Take a moment to reflect on your life.

Now smile at all the things you overcome. When you thought it is was over you. Yes, you did it when people counted you out, just when you thought you lost you and your mind. Oh yes, you all that and some mo'!! God is good! Right?

It's incredible the things life throws at us and the "We cannot change the cards we are dealt, just how we play the hand." — Randy Pausch, The Last Lecture I am a young adult thus far in my life the knowledge I gain I used it as strengthen to expand my intellect spiritually and physically. It's the smallest pieces to the puzzle make up the entire picture. Every day God creates a small piece of your puzzle. The puzzle might take some time to create, figure out, and even find. It's okay. I say all this to say we cannot be ruin. We can only be polished.

In my time of misery, I shed light on others, encourage and love one another. If we all come together anything is possible, we can make a difference, build our brothers/ sisters. Sometimes people think the heroic deeds are the most important, but the smallest have the most impact on others. The minor acts usually are the most remembered. I know, we often get upset about circumstances in our lives, but thank God for the things that didn't go according to our plan. The plan we thought was for us could have been our death trap. Until we understand God directs our lives, we'll be okay with whatever we have to face. God always has the last say. No, I don't have all the answers; God continually shows us the signs.

Sometimes I think the words on these pages are just words, but there are my strength, my uniqueness, and my life. When I write, I feel at liberty. I pick the pen up and flow. I know one day these stories will uplift many.

A tool for us find yourself learning something new daily set goals. It will make us grow, develop, and gain it's not just a benefit. Every day make it a duty to write; express yourself. It may help someone who may be in the same shoes we are one day. Try to be a rainbow someone's cloud as Maya Angelo states. Music keeps us all sane and words give us courage and solidity. Take every day a step at a time. We cannot make anything happen with worries, so take steps back and be productive.

As the years have passed in my life, I found out we can say all we are going to do, but with no action, its imagination drawn with I need too, should haves, I could haves, and so forth. DO NOT let your imagination be a vision with no mission or I'll say lousy reality. In life, we must go through the season(s) of God (breaking and pressing/pruning of us). We hate; it only makes us appreciate what it took to get there, or we'll lose it all.

Chapter 5
Plan

Plan

a: a method for achieving an end
b: an often-customary method of doing something: PROCEDURE
c: an orderly arrangement of parts of an overall design or objective – Merriam-Webster Dictionary

Let those definitions sink in. Read them about 3 more times. Okay, are you ready?

P-L-A-N
Plan is a powerful word. I'm going to break it down.
P is for position. We have to realize we cannot follow our plan, but we can follow God's plan. While we follow it, we have to trust God an let him POSITION is in the plan. However, we got to let God intervene. Which bring us to L.

L is for lead. We have to let God take the lead and remove our hands. ". . . 'Not by might nor by power, but by my Spirit,' says the LORD Almighty." Zechariah 4:6 When letting God lead we have no worries the road may seem bumpy, but it for our good to motivate for A. A is for achievement. We have to achieve to get the destiny God has PLANNED for our lives.

N is for now. We for to get into POSITION to let God LEAD us so that we can ACHIEVE his plan. NOW go forth. The plan we try to set push us back. They stop us in our tracks, but with his plan, he will give us the fruit of the land. "If ye be willing and obedient, ye shall eat the good of the land:" Isaiah 1:19 KJV.

I can assure you all I know it is hard to stay focus. We often feel like things aren't working. We seek out actions to benefit us, but it makes things ten times worst. We tend to change the entire plan which makes us forget about the original blueprint. These things steer us away from purpose resulting in being delayed. We react in disobedience which puts all the prayer and fasting in vain. Now we to start over and fight way harder than before. We must pray longer, read the word more, and fast more. Trust the plan of God stay focused, watch as well as pray. In the process of it all, we must watch what is said spoken. Be silent!

While we are in our season of waiting for things to move in our lives, DO NOT lose sight of the prize. If we know the results of issues we're facing we won't fight, work, nor appreciate it. What we must remember as Bishop TD Jakes, says in the miracle there is always misery. When birthing that baby, it's going to be a process. The labor pains are so intense, hard, and seem as if it is about to take you out. Sometimes you want to lay all in it and die in the birthing seasons. But you know you cannot stop pushing because the miracle is excellent. The miracle is the product of you. The baby you developed is your lifeline. God let all the pain, kicks, late nights, and early mornings dwell in life to deliver.

Some situations are comfortable in life, others you got to labor with that thing and delivery that baby. Spiritual warfare is s heavy, but if it is greatness in the result, we will never understand how precious the miracle is. God won't let us rest very hour in the midnight hours he will bother us until it comes forth. It is all for his glory, be obedient, follows the command the first time because the second time it will be harder. Some season is hard to get back. Pass the test the first time! He is preparing us for the next dimension. Pray without ceasing, as well as fasting. We must understand the power of power. We can go in the spiritual rim and get what we need and want. Pull on all the oil, more anointing, and promises of God for us. When we fast, the waters break to plant the seed. Through we pray and fast it all happens in God's timing. We cannot rush God he knows he can trust us enough to allow more blessings to come forth. Give God time hide in the secret place and watch God.

Chapter 6
The Shift

Many obstacles in life are for us to get to our next level. Although they may be hard, they make us stronger and prepare us for the battlefield in the spiritual war of the wickedness. Perseverance is the key. Every day is a challenge to in our faith, pass the test no matter how challenging. When the anointing is on your life, it's not easy it may be times when you feel like hiding in a box or merely running away due to the pressure of life. We cannot see through the blessing it feels like a mistake a big X or we went the wrong way, but when the anointing is great, the devil fights on every end to make us shut up and drawback. Nothing in life is giving it must be earned. And when we go through and sacrifice, we are going to feel the kicks of pressing. But if not, are we sacrificing? Do you know your value?

We sometimes feel like we are losing our minds. If the enemy got our minds, he has us. He doesn't want our cars, money, house, kids. He wants and knows our value. Know your worth women, man, girl, boy!! If we know, we won't allow the mediocre to conflict our minds. Love yourself; we have pep talks with ourselves. Yes, talk to yourself; encouragement elevates. ". . . And calleth those things which be not as though they were." Romans 4:17 KJV. Thank God for the new things speak them into existence. The tongue is a powerful weapon as many people say you are what you eat and you are what you say and also have what you say. We should to close our mouth sometimes and say nothing to confuse our current situation.

Will you say yes after the storm? Will you go through the storm again to get what God has for you? He created it just for you. He loves us even in the storm. We can't see through the storm the clouds are fluffy, and the rain is too heavy, God is forever present. We have to walk it out by faith.

Just a quick deviation I DO NOT want by any means to seem all religious. But I must say when God is the air you breathe, the strength you have, and you tired of enemy continually fighting you. I can go on and go. Trust me; you'll get to a place where all you want is God an everything attached to him and nothing more. We must realize that.

Previously in this chapter, I spoke of the storm, and inevitably the story hit me like a strong wind in the face. My best friend passed away; I could not believe it. I was devasted. I questioned & questioned God I just could not understand. I asked, "Oh Lord how could you take her from me." Especially with me trying to follow the will of God. I was on a day fast, straight my very first time. I was watching a sermon about praying then things to tend to get worse. My oh my got worse for me. Here, I was following God's voice, and he snatched my best friend more so sister after 25 years. This was the first time in my life I experienced death and grieving. I became bitter; the enemy wanted me to fall. I was low. I got to a place where I started to move back from church, bible study, and any association. I was mad. I was BIG mad; I become resentful. Depression overpowered me. I sat in the house hours upon hours sobbing. A cry and pain I never could explain.

Months passed by and I began to come around just a little, but I am still working on my emotions. I didn't know God was trying to show me he is God and he giveth and he taketh away. "And said, Naked came I out of my mother's womb,

NOW THAT YOU KNOW

and naked shall I return thither: the LORD gave, and the LORD hath taken away; blessed be the name of the LORD." Job 1:21 KJV

Only for a time God allowed me to have my friend to push and shake something in my spiritually. She was love; she was sweet as a peach. But through the hard times and grieving, he had a plan for me. God knows the path he wants us to follow and what mountain he wants us to climb. God was placing pressure on me as high as possible. In the making of creating a diamond. Diamonds can only be CUT, but NOT broken. There's always pieces and pieces of diamonds here and there that shines brightly near or far like a star. God got me to a place when I was alone he wanted me to himself; to focus on his moves, spirits, and voice.

In a million years I didn't ever think my life would shift. The shift was a bittersweet shift I miss my best friend, but I know she is in a better place. God moved me to a higher dimension physically but most importantly spiritually. So what's next?!

Self – Care

Drink water

Listen to music

Pray

Change your environment

Start a project

Pamper yourself

Be YOU. Do YOU. ♡ YOU

NOW THAT YOU KNOW

Prayers

_____

_____

_____

_____

_____

_____

_____

_____

_____

_____

_____

_____

_____

_____

_____

_____

NOW THAT YOU KNOW

NOW THAT YOU KNOW

NOW THAT YOU KNOW

NOW THAT YOU KNOW

NOW THAT YOU KNOW

Notes

_____

_____

_____

_____

_____

_____

_____

_____

_____

_____

_____

_____

_____

_____

_____

_____

NOW THAT YOU KNOW

_____

_____

_____

_____

_____

_____

_____

_____

_____

_____

_____

_____

_____

_____

_____

_____

_____

_____

_____

NOW THAT YOU KNOW

NOW THAT YOU KNOW

NOW THAT YOU KNOW

NOW THAT YOU KNOW